SWEET SOUTHERN DAYS

Compiled by
Mary Webb Wray
Frank Alexander Wray

Order this book online at www.trafford.com
or email orders@trafford.com

Most Trafford titles are also available at major online book retailers.

Printed in Victoria, BC, Canada.

ISBN: 978-1-4269-3068-3 (sc)
ISBN: 978-1-4269-3090-4 (e-book)

Library of Congress Control Number: 2010904842

Our mission is to efficiently provide the world's finest, most comprehensive book publishing service, enabling every author to experience success. To find out how to publish your book, your way, and have it available worldwide, visit us online at www.trafford.com

Trafford rev. 4/19/2010

 www.trafford.com

North America & international
toll-free: 1 888 232 4444 (USA & Canada)
phone: 250 383 6864 ✦ fax: 812 355 4082

In Loving Memory Of
Mom

Mary Webb

Other Books by
Frank Alexander Wray
Songs Unspoken
(Volume 1)

Shadow Dawn

When Clowns Cry

The Journal of Martha Wayles Robertson

CONTENTS

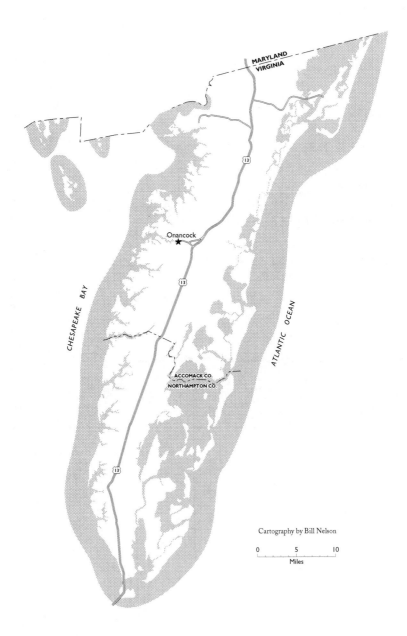

MARYLAND

VIRGINIA

Onancock
★

CHESAPEAKE BAY

ATLANTIC OCEAN

13

13

ACCOMACK CO.
NORTHAMPTON CO.

13

Cartography by Bill Nelson

0   5   10
Miles

X

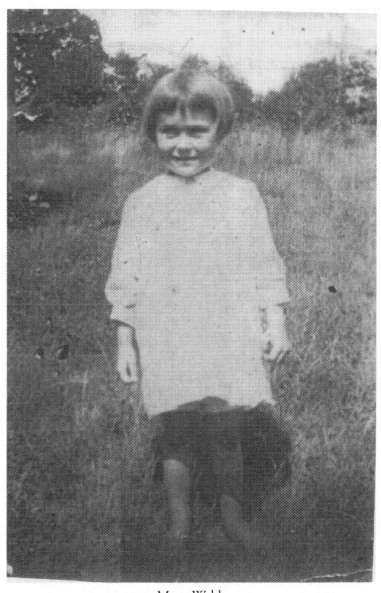

Mary Webb
age 4

FORWARD

It gives me great honor to write the forward to this book titled, SWEET SOUTHERN DAYS, by Mary Adelaide Webb Wray. There is no introduction to this book or epilogue. After all why should it be as it is a book of memoirs written from the heart of my late mom in 2008. Why should there be an epilogue as she died January 21, 2010. Within these pages there are special words written by a lady of wisdom for others to gain knowledge in a troubled world. These are words which can be considered a gift to mankind so a direction will be given to make one's journey a little easier.

It is often said, a picture is worth a thousand words. How true when viewing the picture on the cover of this book. My mother is posed on the cover on the front row to the left and her brother, Lewis, is to her right and other family children all around them. This is the family Webb circle who grew up which seemed to be a far away place in Virginia with very little during the Depression but as mom often said to me,"we never knew as children we had very little because we were so happy."

Mary Adelaide Webb Wray, was born July 1, 1917 in the small but quaint southern town of Boydton, Virginia. This is a town of about 400 people nestled close to the North Carolina and Virginia border. She was the daughter of two loving parents, Lewis Presley Webb and Sally Robertson Webb. All together there were six girls and one boy that God had given to bless this Christian home. In the early years this family circle was broken with the tragic death of a sister, Little Margaret Webb, and it occurred well before her tenth year of life. Throughout the years this heartwarming family circle has been broken many times here on earth until the last one left was my mother, Mary Adelaide Webb Wray. Now, once again this loving Christian home is reunited in Heaven as Mary has provided the last binding link.

Mary has said through the years there was no brighter light than the one that pierced through the tall cedars and for some unknown reason it seemed to her the freedom of the light danced its way gracefully up Cedar Lane to the old homeplace.

It was here along this "HILL" it all started for Mary and it was here she learned at a very early age the love for God, her family, her church, and her country. She was always so proud to say to everybody she met, never once in her life could she ever remember having a family argument but only remembers a special binding love. It was here she learned to face life's challenges with an open mind and to live life in peace. Many times she would mention her home in Boydton, Virginia and she would say," how could anyone forget the homeplace in the south with its hot and humid summer days, beautiful wrought iron fences, Mama and Papa, sisters and brother, and the daily teachings of God.

Many in her family would say how beautiful she sewed and her mother taught her that craft when only twelve years of age. Her quiet ways, her sweet smile, her charming unselfish ways seemed to attract others and often she would be surrounded by many who felt a sincerity of compassion. She resided in Boydton, Virginia for all of her childhood years until completing high school. Yes, it was here in this special place in the world Mary learned from her parents the importance of making a happy Christian home, sharing, caring, Christian love, and the necessary tools for survival by helping her fellowman and this gift she passed to her children and grandchildren.

It was on the Historical Eastern Shore of Virginia in the small town of Onancock, Virginia a town only a few miles from the Chesapeake Bay and a few miles from the Atlantic Ocean, Mary resided for a period of over 65 years with her loving husband, Frank (Pete) Wray. She did her very best to serve her church and her community and to be a loving and supportive wife and mother and grandmother. She certainly exceeded her devotions and expectations to so many throughout her long life's journey in a quiet and lady-like manner here on earth and now she is continuing her loving and unselfish ways in Heaven and has now provided the missing link to once again complete the family circle God had created and is now with her loved ones.

There are many accomplishments my mother acquired during her life but one in particular is this little book she wrote. It was written at the end of her life which makes it more special to me. She never gave up on life and never took a defeated attitude but looked at life as a learning experience and no matter how consumed one may be by negative events of the world she always looked for the good in life and kept a positive attitude. In later life her expression was,"I know more loved ones THERE than here." SWEET SOUTHERN DAYS is a special book written by a special lady, my mom, who only looked for the best in everything.

FRANK ALEXANDER WRAY
xxxxxxxxxxxxxxxxxxxxxxxxxxxxxxxxxxxxxxxxxxxxxxxxxxxxxxxx

Home on the Hill

Mama and Papa Webb

"TIME IS FOR ONCE BUT, GONE FOREVER."
Frank Alexander Wray

A SPECIAL THANK-YOU

There is only one person that comes to mind to receive a sincere thank -you of appreciation for the outcome of this book titled, SWEET SOUTHERN DAYS. That person is my sister, Carol Anne Wray Barrineau who for many months did everything she could to write down things my mother told her, to correct my mother's mistakes, and mom was elderly, and to put the words in their proper place. Without her there would be no story for Mary Wray to tell and surely nothing for the reader. Yet, because of Carol's unselfish ways she was able to do her very best to put this story in front of the reader. That is not only unselfish but and act of true love for a parent. Thank -you Carol Anne Wray Barrineau and it is a special one.

A THOUGHT

Youth is not a time of life—it is a state of mind. Nobody grows old by merely living a number of years; people grow old only by deserting their ideals. Years wrinkle this skin, but to give up enthusiasm wrinkles the soul. Worry, doubt, self-distrust, fear and despair: these are the long, long years that bow the head and turn the growing spirit back to dust.

Whether 110 or 10, there is in every human being's heart the love of wonder, the sweet amazement of stars and star like things and thoughts, the undaunted challenges of events in everyone's life, the unfailing child-like appetite for what next, and the job and the evergoing game of life.

Yes, you are as young as your faith, as old as your doubt, as young as your self-confidence, as old as your fear, as young as your hope, as old as your despair. Yes, you are very young.

My state of mind tells me I am still young even though some will say to me, "Mary, I cannot believe your age." Why should I care about my age because God Almighty is not yet finished with me. Perhaps I can still touch a life in a positive way or still feel the tender touch of a child or feel the warm arms of one of my children around me on a lonely day that may give a ray of sunshine. A flower created by God and its beauty forever does not like to be stomped upon and taken from this earthly scene nor does humanity of all ages. Life is precious and I thank Him as He is blessing me as He has always done for me.

_____M.W.W.

Mary Webb
age 12

Left to Right: Mary, Sarah, Lewis, Nell, Virginia, and Bess

THE WEBB CHILDREN

MY parents: Lewis Presley Webb and Sally Robertson were Married by Mr. J. T. Sewell, April 14, 1909

1. Sara Robertson Webb, born April 25, 1910 on Monday night at 10 pm at the homeplace in Boydton, Virginia, and she weighed 8 ½ lbs, baptized at Mrs. Laird's by Dr. Smart.
2. Margaret Miller Webb, born September 29, 1911 on Friday 7am and she weighed 8 ¼ lb, baptized March 12, 1912 by Dr. Smart.
3. Nell Wayles Webb, born June 16, 1913 at 7:30 pm, weighed 10 pounds, baptized n Mrs. Laird's arms at her home by Mr. Scott on November 22, 1913.
4. Lewis Presley Webb, born March 16, 1915, weighed 9 ½ lbs, baptized by Mr. Kabler.
5. Mary Adelaide Webb, born July I, 1917 on Sunday at 7am, weighed 8 pounds, baptized by Dr.. Whitney.
6. Bess Johnson Webb, born June 22, 1919, baptized by Dr. Whitney.
7. Virginia Laird Webb, born February 22, 1921, baptized by Dr. Whitney.

xxxxxxxxxxxxxxxxxxxxxxxxxxxxxxxxxxxxxxxxxxxxxxxxxxxxx

MARY WEBB WRAY and FRANK ALEXANDER WRAY

MY TREASURES

God moves in a mysterious way
His wonders to perform
He plants His footsteps in the sea,
And rides upon the storm.

His purpose will ripen fast,
Unfolding every hour,
the bud may have a bitter taste,
But sweet will be the flowers.
_____W. Cowper
How wonderful are His ways_____M.W.W.

Humans have 46 chromosomes, each animal has its own
number.
_____Quest Magazine

Glimpse of Heaven

Isaiah-30-26.
Isaiah 60-19-20.
Revelation-21-23.

Left to Right: Virginia, Lewis, Bess, Nell, Mary

HOW THESE MEMORIES
FLOOD MY SOUL...

*Memoirs compiled by Mary Adelaide Webb Wray, January 2008
as Mom told them to me, Carol Ann Wray Barrineau*

We children knew that all was well when we would see Mama and Daddy sitting in each other's laps in the kitchen.

Words were not spoken, but I knew Daddy knew we wondered why we didn't have money like other children did. Daddy said, "We don't have money, but we have blue blood running through our veins. For a long time, I thought our blood was blue! Then Daddy would say, "Our lineage goes back to George Washington, and we have records to prove it." And Mama would say that on her Robertson side, their lineage went back to Robert the Bruce, King of Scotland (in the year 1320); (I have the papers in my trunk showing our lineage goes back to these dates).

Daddy always put his coppers (pennies) on the mantel in their room. I took a few coppers and bought a few pieces of candy for Mama and me. Mama sat at her sewing machine so much and I thought it would give her a boost. I knew Nell would sweep the front porch so before she swept, I planted the coppers at the front porch in the red clay dirt. I went out and dug up the coppers while Nell was sweeping. I said, "Nell, look what I found!" Nell said, "Mary, you are the luckiest thing I ever saw." I didn't tell her the truth until we were teenagers.

There were six of us: five girls and one boy, the one lonely boy. There used to be seven of us, but little Margaret died when she was 8 years old. We were all born at home, a home built on a hill. My grandfather, Dr. Robert T. Webb, was the overseer, and the home was just one mile out of the county seat (Mecklenburg) of Boydton, Virginia.

Nell had a photo album. I took a picture of me out of her book for my boyfriend and she didn't like that and fussed with me. That was bad, but the worse thing was when I dug up her moss rose bush, thinking it was a weed! She was so mad that I could see the veins come up in her neck--then I knew she was mad--but she forgave me.

My oldest sister, Sara, was a little bossy. I stood right in the middle of the back yard and proclaimed as loud as I could to the world and to Sara: "You may be the boss of the barnyard, but you "ain't" the boss of me!"

When it was my time to wash dishes, I wouldn't wipe off a place for my sister to put the clean dishes. Not until my sister would call Mama from the next room: "Mama, Mary won't wipe off a place to put the dishes."

Mama would say, "Mary, wipe off a place," then I would do it. Mama was my only boss.

I must have been mighty stubborn, even with Mama. I had to hang out the washed clothes on the clothes line and any where I could find a place to hang them: on the fence, on the bushes—

anywhere. She asked me to hang out a week's clothes for 8 people on Saturday. No way would I do it! She then asked me to get a switch from the peach tree. I took my own dear sweet time. I went in the house with a tiny switch and when Mama saw it, she laughed and hugged me. I hung out the clothes to dry...

When Mama was a child, she used to ride in a horse-drawn sleigh.

We stood behind Daddy while he shoveled the snow from our home to the highway so we could walk the mile to school.

One summer, Dick Lewis, a traveling comedian, would come to Boydton. One particular time was in 1927. When the show was over, it was pitch black and we had that 1 mile walk to home. There was Lewis, Bess, Virginia, and me. Lewis had just gotten some long, white sailor bell-bottom pants. They were real wide at the bottom. We were running home. I could beat Lewis running, because his pants kept wrapping around his legs and I giggled to myself. Years later, I asked Lewis why he didn't protect us. He said that he was just as afraid as we were!

Bolling Robertson, my cousin from Petersburg, and I were the same age. He grew up to become a missionary in Liberia, Africa, for all his adult life. His mother mailed us a cute picture of his sister, Mary Evelyn and Bolling and in the picture, Mary Evelyn was standing by a pony and Bolling was sitting on the pony. Well, I was jealous and tore that picture up! Of course, I had to admit it to Mama--I was the guilty one. Mama whipped me, I guess, but I don't remember her doing it.

When Bolling and I were 14 years old, I asked Bolling to say the Books of the Bible from memory. He said every one, without hesitating, and I knew right then that he was going to be a man of God

Mr. & Mrs. Thompson's farm joined ours. They had children and one son, Ray, and I played together; both of us were 8 years old. We were playing around their open well and I wanted some water. A new bucket was at the end of the rope. I was holding on to the bucket, but the latch wouldn't hold. I was holding on tight. As I stood on my tip-toes, I could feel myself going in the well. Ray pulled me back. Now, I think it had to be an angel. I skinned my arm real bad with the rope going so fast and when I went home Mama asked what happened to my arm. I told her that Ray hit me with a plank as I didn't want her to know what really happened. So Mama marched herself to Mrs. Thompson's and asked why Ray did this. Mrs. Thompson told her the truth. Mama came back home and questioned me. She didn't fuss with me because, I guess, she was so happy I didn't go in the well.

Alberta Hill lived on the property; she named her daughter Mary after me. Alberta and her husband would come to see us on Saturday night and he would play his guitar and sing to us. We pulled up chairs in the hallway to listen. He played and sang beautiful songs.

When Mama closed her old foot-pedal sewing machine up, we used it as a dressing table to "primp." She later got a new foot-pedal sewing machine.

When I became a teenager, I used to dream about falling in a well so many times. I would sit right up in bed thinking about the dream, then go back to sleep, so happy it was only a dream.

Mama made our dresses and underwear with chicken feed bags and she made Lewis' underwear with them, too. We'd wear our pretty dresses that Mama made to church and school.

When I was around 7 years old, I put a piece of grass in my mouth and the blade of grass slid down my throat, stopping midway. I told Lewis that I had a piece of "grass" in my throat and he took my hand and we both ran home to Mama. Lewis told Mama that I had a piece of "glass" in my throat but Mama knew that I had said "grass" and not "glass." Mama gave me a piece of bread and water and I swallowed the blade of grass.

During recess at school, we would play "snap the whip." Everyone would hold hands, forming a circle, and then run around and around. After a while, people would let go of the other's hand until there was only one person left.

When Sara was 18 and before she went to nursing school in Baltimore, Stewart Hawkins sold us our first washing machine, a Maytag. Before we had our Maytag, we would wash clothes using a wash board and a big tub. Stewart Hawkins came to the house and he liked Sara. He liked to sing and as they were walking around the house, he would hold Sara around her waist singing, "Girl of My Dreams, I Love You."

After school and when it was warm, we would stop by the town yard spring and drink water from the spring using our tin folding cups. We would leave the cups at the spring and after school, we would drink the water. First, though, we had to run the tadpoles away before filling our tin cups with water. We each had our own cup.

On the other side of Webb's Creek and close to an old chimney and abandoned piece of land, we would pick blackberries from wild bushes. There were snakes there but they never bothered us; there were surely Angels around us. We would take the blackberries home to Mama for her to make blackberry dumplings and then she would make a sugar sauce to put on the blackberry dumplings. Mama was always happy when we would bring her the berries.

I was 8 years old and was walking on the path to home from the main road, and I heard the sound of a rattlesnake close by me. I ran as fast as I could up the path to home.

Another time when I was 8 years old, we used to play under a culvert and wade in the water. One day, I saw a water moccasin swimming in the water. I found a nice size rock and killed the dog-gone thing! I told Mama about seeing the snake and she asked me if I killed it and I said, "Yes." Mama and Daddy had so much faith because they knew their children were safe from all evil. We never had any fear of anyone or anything harming us when we walked to town and back.

At the Boydton Presbyterian Church, there would be black men standing on the sidewalk. When we would get close to them, they would move to the grass and stand there, tipping their hats at us as we walked by.

The potatoes we raised in the summer were harvested in the fall. We took them upstairs and put them in a large room above Mama and Daddy's bedroom downstairs. We would eat potatoes during the long, cold winter months and also feed the farmhands potatoes. All those potatoes piled up over Mama and Daddy's bedroom! It was a miracle that the floor never gave way with all the weight of the potatoes. After the potatoes were gone, we swept the floor and, using a piece of chalk, we would draw three lines to divide the room among Bess, Virginia, and me. Because we divided the room into three lines, we each had our own dollhouse. We pretended to visit each other with our dolls. While the other wasn't looking, we'd wet each other's dolls. Later, we'd go in the front yard with our dolls and play some more. We'd knock on a tree and visit each other with our dolls.

When we harvested tomatoes, we'd go in the garden with a wheel barrow. Smiling and laughing, we wheeled the tomatoes to the back door, took the tomatoes out, and put them on the kitchen table. We'd wash and peel them and Mama would boil them. We had a metal kitchen table and, not realizing what would happen, I put a hot, filled jar of the tomatoes on the table and the jar exploded. Mama didn't fuss with me but I learned a lesson!

My job before school was to let Mama's chickens out of the chicken house that was under the pear tree. I skipped to the chicken house. On my way, something happened. A gush of wind came to my right ear and a strong voice within the wind said, "You don't love God, you love me!" I murmured, "Yes I do love God!" For two mornings in a row, I heard the same thing, and then it left me.

Later in life, Pete and I had a good Christian friend, Mr. Albert Adolfson, and I asked him if this ever happened to him. He said no, but he had heard of people who had similar experiences.

We used to go to Mason's Lake, a lake not far from home. There was a floating float. As I was sitting on it, two young adults jumped on one end of the float. This caused me to slide off into the water, way over my head. I saw Mr. Mason starting to take his pants off to rescue me, but two younger boys rescued me.

Another time at Mason's Lake, I saw two of the most beautiful young teenagers walking out in the water, knee deep. I thought they had fallen from the sky (just kidding)! Later, I found out they were from Wilson, North Carolina. The brunet was Ava Gardner and I never did know who the blonde was. I knew who the brunet was, though. Ava Gardner was buried right there in Wilson, North Carolina.

At a quarry in Baltimore and not knowing it was a quarry, another couple, Pete, and I went off by ourselves to go swimming. They went hand-in-hand to waters edge and I sat down and watched them walk. They said I was a sissy. I kept looking, and all 3 just disappeared. I kept looking, walking out to where I last saw them. Then Pete hollered to me for me to call for help. I ran over a hill and hollowed for help. Two young men ran and pulled them out of the water. The girl couldn't swim and was pulling Pete and the other man down in the deep water with her. We found out that the quarry was so deep that they didn't know exactly how deep it was. After that, the quarry was fenced off. I know angels were with us.

Barier and Margaret Ann Adams had a small boat and they would take Pete and me fishing. On one fishing trip, you couldn't see land on either side. The fish were biting like crazy, so we were having a good time. All of a sudden, a bad storm came up and we were stuck. It was an electrical storm and we had no life vests on the boat. They were laughing at me because my hair was standing up straight on my head and the boat was rocking and they were catching fish! When we got back on land, I told them that I would never get in a small boat again, and I never did.

There is something grand and glorious in viewing the "glow to early morn." The feathered songsters make the air vocal with their notes of praise to the Great Creator (from Mary Epps Robertson's composition book, 1858).

When I was a child, there was a man who lived in the back woods not far from home. His name was Ransom Kanichet. We were afraid of him, but Mama wasn't. Ransom Kanichet would open the kitchen stove oven, get a hot sweet potato, and swallow it whole. You could see it go down his throat. He was so hungry. It was a sight to behold! Mama would give him clean clothes and tell him to go in the ditch, take off his dirty clothes and leave them in the ditch and put on the clean clothes. There was a path from our house and the main road. We got Jack, our dog, in on the act by telling Jack to sic 'em. We said sic 'em real loud. You should have seen Ransom running down that path! We said that he was running so fast that we could play marbles on his coat tails!

Daddy asked me to go with him and plant the garden in the "bottom." I didn't want to because Bess and Virginia got to stay home. I was 12 years old. I looked and saw Bess and Virginia running down the hill with a picture in Bess' hand. It was the first picture of Jimmy Jr. we had seen; he was 6 months old. I didn't want to put my hands on the picture because my hands were dirty from planting tomatoes. Daddy was so sweet talking to me as we worked. I didn't say much to Daddy because I was peeved with Bess and Virginia. Now, I'm so ashamed of myself!

Sara, our oldest sister, moved to far-away Baltimore to go in training to become a nurse. Before she left, Bess, Virginia, and I wanted something to remember her by so we asked her if we could have a little bit of her hair. "Yes," she said. This made us happy.

Lewis had a rope around his waist and the other end of the rope was around the cow's neck. The cow saw a pretty patch of green grass and took off running fast. Lewis was on the ground being dragged by the cow, going through a pile of broken glass and remnants of debris from when Grandmother and Grandfather lived at the house earlier. Finally, the cow stopped. Lewis had scratches all over his body. It was during the summer, and he stayed on a cot on the front porch to recuperate. Mama put Calamine Lotion on him and, thankfully, he had no broken bones.

Lewis would run home from school with his head lowered, playing like he was a choo-choo train. One day, people had put a barb wire fence up and he didn't know it was there. Well, the barb wire cut one cheek wide open--you could see his teeth. The country doctor worked on his face and it healed up very well.

A lady up town told everybody that the Webb's have more trouble than anyone she knew of. Well, this lady had nine children. Before she died at age 92, she had lost one-half of her children.

When Daddy's glasses got so dirty and he tried to read the newspaper that he got from Lucy, Helen, and Ola Bevell, I would take his glasses off his face, take them in the kitchen and wash them off, and then put them back on his face.

After it rained, the T-Model Ford couldn't get up the slippery, red-clay hill. Bess, Virginia, and I would get out of the car, get behind it, and push it up the hill while Daddy was steering it. Then, the three of us would get back in the T-Model Ford and go home. A lot of times, when we would ride to town, we'd take our dolls with us so the dolls could see the scenery.

When we went to Buffalo Lithia Springs, we usually had several flat tires. Every summer, we'd go to Buffalo Lithia Springs in Buffalo, Virginia where dances were held. Bess, who was 10 years old, Virginia, who was 8, and I, who was 12, would sneak on the dance floor and dance between the teenage dancers; we would be squatting down. Mama and Daddy would be in rocking chairs on the front porch laughing and talking to the visitors, not knowing what the three of us were doing.

Daddy never got mad or angry with his children except for one time with Lewis. Daddy said he was going to whip Lewis for something he did and I can't remember what it was. So while Daddy was holding Lewis' hand, the two of them kept going round and round in a circle, and Daddy never did get to whip Lewis. While they were doing this, we were looking out of the kitchen window laughing--Mama, too. And there they were:

Daddy and Lewis going round and round. Instead of Daddy showing his temper, he would go outside and kick the mule, but he didn't hurt the mule because it was a gentle kick.

Daddy never showed his temper to Mama, in spite of the turmoil of the depression, trying to provide for his family, and providing for the farm hands. Every night, Daddy and Mama would kiss the children goodnight.

Every Saturday, Daddy walked the mile to town to buy staples. He would always bring back for us fig newtons. He'd wake us up to give us a fig newton and then we'd go back to sleep.

Christmas morning, we'd wake up with soot on our pillow cases where, we learned later, Daddy had put his hands in soot to put on our pillow cases to let us know that Santa had been there. Christmas morning, we'd have an apple at the toe, an orange at the heel, and dried raisins and hard candy in between one of Mama's stockings. A doll was always at the top of the stocking. We saved the money from picking cotton to buy a ball, yo-yo, and toy watch to give to each other. Christmas Eve, we would be laughing and happy while we were stretching Mama's stockings because we wanted Santa to fill them up. We were all laughing but Mama wasn't because she knew there wouldn't be much to fill our stockings. We'd go to the woods to cut a tree. It was Bess' job to replace the burned-out Christmas bulbs on the tree. These bulbs were the very big kind.

Mr. Hermie Williams owned a jewelry store in Richmond. He knew us because his daddy was a preacher in Mama's church and she knew his family when she was growing up. We called him "Miss Hermie" because of all the diamonds he would wear. He would visit us on the hill. We used to be so proud when we would see him at school in his big car to pick us up and take us home. He'd blow the horn for us. Before we had a radio and Amos and

Andy was very popular, we'd go in a shed at home and sit on the back seat of "Miss Hermie's" car and listen to Amos and Andy.

When Bess was a toddler, we were all busy in the house and no one missed Bess. We realized that Bess wasn't in the house so we looked for her and finally found her sleeping in the hay in the stable. Everyone was overjoyed to find her safe and sound.

The first time Pete went to Boydton, my sisters thought that he was the best looking man they had ever seen. Pete, being born and raised in Norristown, Pennsylvania, thought everyone in Virginia was happy-go-lucky like we were. Pete made a hit with my sisters and there are pictures to prove it. In an affectionate way, he called Mama "battle-ax" and Mama loved to be called that by him because she knew it was his way of saying that he cared for her.

Close to home was a dirt road that led to a creek. We walked on that dirt road and through the woods, never realizing that there might be snakes or anything else that could harm us--we were just happy--going to the creek.

Ranson Kanichet lived close to it. One side of the creek was deeper than the other. We would fill our buckets with water to take home to the garden to water the tomatoes and potatoes. Sometimes, before leaving, we would go wading in the water. Bess had her small doll and she accidentally dropped it in the water and it floated away in the deep water. Bess stood crying for her doll because we couldn't retrieve it in the deep water.

In the summer, Bolling and other teenage friends from town would go to the creek to wade in the shallow water. We took a picture in our bathing suits of Bolling, Nell, Bess, Virginia, Lewis, and me. From that time on, the creek was known as "Webb's Creek."

Daddy took us swimming and wading at another place close to home on Sunday's using Mr. Thompson's Touring Studebaker. One time, Mr. Thompson was driving with Daddy in the front and Bess, Virginia, Lewis, and me in the back along with three of Mr. Thompson's four children. When we got out of the water, we were full of leeches on our bodies. Daddy had a hard time trying to get the leeches off us.

Nell, Virginia, Bess, and I slept in the big bedroom upstairs. I was around 10 years old when this happened--the walls were white without any "stick people" or pictures on the walls. I don't know who it was that came up with the idea but this is what happened: we got Daddy's tar bucket that he used to patch up the leaking roof, went to the chicken house, and got three of the longest chicken feathers we could find, and took these things to our bedroom upstairs. As high as we could reach, we started to draw our magnificent "stick people." Either Nell or Sara told on us and told Mama! I'm not for certain, but I think we had to stand in line while Mama gave us a very light whipping. Those "stick people" stayed on our bedroom walls for years, mainly because we didn't have money to buy the paint to paint over our "stick people."

While Daddy was getting ready for Church, he would be humming "The Old Rugged Cross" as he was shaving. He wouldn't let any of us around him when he was shaving with his straight razor. He was afraid that he would accidentally cut himself while using the straight razor. We were faithful about going to Church every Sunday and all of us would walk to the Boydton Methodist Church and Sunday school if we didn't have a cold. Mama sang in the choir, with much feeling in her singing.

We loved playing hide and seek. When we were ready to "seek," we would say, "Who dot said who dot when I say who dot?"

A teenage boy used to milk the cow. Daddy asked him if he got all of the milk. The young boy said, "I got all she strut!"

As children, Bess and I went to see Mrs. Turpin and she asked what we had for dinner. I said, "con puddin" and Bess said, "Mary, not con puddin, but norn mudden!"

Billy Starns would bring wood into the house and Mama would feed him. He was retarded but gentle and wouldn't hurt anyone. He would eat Mama's stew and Mama would ask Billy how he liked her stew. Billy said, "Better than noughting."

We lost a sill under the house because of dancing in the living room. Our Gone with the Wind oil lamp on top of the piano was dancing, too!

Bess and I sat in a double seat in one class room. "Put all papers away," the teacher said. Bess forgot to put her papers away. The teacher told her to stay after school. I told the teacher that we had a witness. He asked "Who?" I said, "God." Well, Daddy, who carried the lantern, Bess, and I went up town to see Mr. Brien, the principal. Daddy told the principal that he knew his children didn't cheat. The next day, Bess took the test over and got a grade of 98.

Uncle William, who was Daddy's brother, and Daddy used to play together. When they were little boys, Will was sick. Daddy got on his knees and prayed to God to please make Will well because he 'wasn't near through playing with Will yet.'

Mrs. Long, our neighbor, was always feeling poorly. We children would ask Mrs. Long how she felt, and she always said poorly, very poorly. She and Mama were the same age and she lived 10 years longer than Mama.

We used to walk to Webb's Creek and on the way was a hollow tree. Nell and her friend, Irene Long, were in front of me, and I heard them talking about the stork leaving babies in the hollow tree. They were questioning each other about that. A mystery--I didn't say a word. I guess I was around 6 years old and they were around 10 years old.

Virginia was chosen to represent Boydton one year for the Tobacco Festival. She looked so pretty on the float. Mama and I went to South Boston to see the parade (I have pictures to prove it!). Harriett Pillett Bales represented Clarksville. (Virginia was also chosen to be Miss Boydton.) A big dance was held in a tobacco warehouse in South Boston that night. Guy Lombardo's orchestra played. It was a thrilling night and so many people were there.

Lewis and Bess were in a talent show in Chase City and Lewis played his mouth organ while Bess did the Charleston. The tune that Lewis played was "Yes, Sir, That's My Baby." They had so much talent. This was during the boogie-woogie era.

I don't know how this worked, but it did. Lewis would string a piece of wire from the back porch to the stable, and we would talk to each other over this wire.

Lewis was riding his bike and saw a pigeon in the ditch with a string around his leg. He brought it home, and we had a pet pigeon. We called the pigeon Penna. Penna would get on Mama's shoulder and stay on her shoulder and watch her sew for a long time.

When Mama would make some extra good food, she would always say, "its rollicking good!"

Daddy and Mr. Chambers Goode were life-long friends. When he died, Lewis told Daddy and Daddy said, "I be dog; I'll have to pack my suitcase!"

Every Christmas morning for breakfast, we had oyster stew. The oysters came up from Norfolk. Sara didn't like oysters, so her oysters went to Daddy.

We had a shed with a tin roof in the back yard. There was a ladder that we climbed onto the roof. After we sliced apples, they were put on the hot roof to dry out. I forget how many days we did this. Then, Mama would take care of them for the winter months to come. She would make some "rollicking" good desserts.

Bess, Virginia, and I would go with Daddy in the wagon to the cotton field and corn field to chop cotton and to weed the corn. We had a "rollicking" good time with Daddy driving the wagon and us in the back, laughing and happy. We worked hard but it didn't hurt us.

Daddy's saw mill was close to home at one time. We would find saplings, pull them down, and ride them pretending they were horses. Oh, what fun we had!

Bess, Virginia, and I sat on the fence at the cow pen while Nell milked the cow. Nell kept our interest while she told us about how one day in the future, she would be rich and buy Mama and Daddy all the luxuries of life.

I had a hand-full of brass buttons that I found outside next to a pile of rotten material, and I asked Mama what they were. Mama said they came off my grandfather's Civil War uniforms. When the War was over, he put the uniforms in an outside building. After putting his Civil War uniforms in an outside building, he never looked at them again.

I was 2 years old when my sister, Margaret, died. We always called her "little Margaret." Every summer, mama would look in her trunk as we stood by. She would let us hold little Margaret's doll and then Mama would put it back in the trunk.

Lightning hit the cedar tree that was right by the dining room window. The tree split right in half. Jimmy Jr. almost got hit by the lightning.

The sawmill engine bolt blew out and steam flowed out. It almost blinded my Daddy and it burned other parts of his body. We were so glad that he recovered from that ordeal!

When we were children, children used to come see us and we would play hid and seek.

Working all morning, we could play croquet in the afternoon. This was in the summer time.

Henrietta and Alberta would come to our back yard and dance the Charleston. They had rhythm. Nothing but red clay was in the back yard.

When I was in the first, second, and third grades, we had to walk by the cow slaughterhouse. Such terrible, mournful sounds would come from inside the slaughterhouse where the cows were killed for human consumption. This was on the old road but when the new road was built, we didn't have to go by the slaughterhouse any more.

A young man, who had recently been released from prison, lived on the other side of Webb's Creek. He would stand on the other side of the creek and watch us play in the water and would talk to us. Amazingly, we were not afraid of him. He said that Virginia was the one he liked. Later in life, I realized that we had angels watching over us and that was why nothing happened to us because we had no idea who the man was.

1927: Alberta and I were playmates. On Good Friday, Alberta and I ran up one hill and down the next. Instead of running down the hill on my feet, I was going so fast that I landed on my left side and broke three bones in my elbow. Going home, and as my elbow was turning all around, I kept telling Alberta not to tell Mama. Dr. Finch, who was a country doctor, fixed my arm. Every week, Daddy took me to Chase City and Dr. Finch would straighten out my arm and put another plaster cast on it. My elbow took about 2 years to heal.

When Nell worked at Virginia Polytechnic Institute (VPI) in Blacksburg, Virginia, she would save her money to buy paint for the house. She, herself, painted the inside of the house and she paid two men to paint the outside. When the outside was completely painted, we would go down the hill and turn around and look at our home on the hill and see how pretty it looked after it was painted.

Early one morning, when I was a child, I looked outside. There was a dusting of snow, just enough to create a beautiful cosmetic effect.

In one of the out-buildings, Daddy put farm equipment in barrels. In one barrel, there was a bee's nest. Bees were swarming all around, and I told everyone to stand still and they wouldn't bother us. Everyone else ran inside except for me and then a bee stung me on my nose! They were all laughing at me! The next day, my nose was swollen and I had to ride the bus back to Baltimore with Adelaide and Carol (Frank wasn't born yet).

Pete and I were married in Boydton in 1938 by my Uncle Robert (Dr. Robert T. Webb). We were the last couple that Uncle Robert married. After we were married, we lived in Baltimore where Adelaide and Carol were born. We left Baltimore and moved to the mountains of Virginia. We later moved to the Eastern Shore of Virginia (Onancock), and Frank was born in Nassawadox, Virginia.

Pete and I reared three delightful children: Mary Adelaide Wray Hollandsworth, Carol Ann Wray Barrineau, and Frank Alexander Wray, Jr.

My accomplishments in life are as follows:

1. Sewed most of my adult life.
2. Worked at the FarmEx.
3. Worked at Byrd's.
4. Picked pine cones
5. I worked at Holly Farms and had pneumonia twice while working there. Dr. Bosworth told me that I had no business working at Holly Farms and that I wasn't cut out for that work.
6. Worked at the Parksley Nursing Home. Kathryn Berry (Pete's sister) gave me her 1-year old blue Buick.
7. Took U.S. Census in 1969.
8. Made a lot of braided rugs.
9. Made Adelaide's wedding gown.
10. Made David's little white suit for Frank's wedding.

Nell told me on the phone that life is bitter-sweet. She was talking about Frank's book, "Shadow Dawn."

No Christian will skip through this life without having problems (Frank said this).

Hebrews 2-14:15:
Forasmuch then as the children are partakers of flesh and blood, He (Jesus) also Himself likewise took part of the same; that through death, He might destroy Him that had the power that is the Devil. And deliver them who through fear of death were all their lifetime subject to bondage.

Frank said this,. He said that there is a saying that "life will never be sweet to the ones who are bitter toward others."

I actually poured my heart out as I assembled these thoughts; it was an urge of the Holy Spirit. I give God the credit, as He is my Divine Teacher.

These sayings, thoughts, and passages will serve as symbols of faith to all of God's people. They are shining examples of a true believer working fervently in God's Vineyard.

Eternity, tho' pleasing, is a dreadful thought.
… Shakespeare

Handful of pills: swallow them and say, 'you go to your respective places.'
…Warner Ray Hargis

I'm not the best, but I'm better than some of the rest.

If you don't use it, you lose it.

We live in our own world—within the world.
… Frank A. Wray

On the Civil War: "They fight for others, sow in tears, for others to reap in joy."
...Mary Adelaide Webb Robertson

Actions speak louder than words.

The descent to avenues (hell) is easy.
...quote from Virgil

To plant a garden is to walk with God.
...Lance Kaufman

Larry King said that his mother would say, "From your lips to God."

Heaven and earth never agreed better to frame a place for man's habitation.
...Captain John Smith referring to the Eastern Shore of Virginia
circa 1608

"Love knows no season." Someone wrote in Bolling's book, "The footprints Bolling has left on the sands of time—follow them."

The same sunshine and rain from Heaven, which produce the flowers and fruit, ministers also to the production of the tares.
...J. Lenoir Chambers

I'd often wonder why the sky is blue. Carol asked Rich Rogers this question, and he explained about molecules in the air and other things but his final answer was, "It could just be that God is a great artist and likes that color next to the sun."

Shakespeare's "Hamlet:" "The world is a stage, and we are all actors."

I Timothy, 6:10
For the love of money is the root of all evil which while some coveted after, they have erred from the faith and pierced themselves through with many sorrows.

December 25, 2007...
Our Lord and Savior Jesus Christ's Birthday is a happy day for so many people, but how very sad for so many of God's loved ones...

Just when we are full of knowledge, we die.

The Webb Family

Revisiting "The Hill"

It's hard to describe the feeling that came over me when Virginia and I recently visited "the hill." This is where our home used to be! The house is torn down now; all that remains is the dairy. Three-fourths of it is cement, the rest of it are weather boards. That's where we kept milk, butter, and canned food that we put up during the summer months. I used to think the dairy was large but it's very small. Daddy let Lewis put his footprint on the step before the cement got hard. Being that Lewis was the only boy, we girls agreed it was Lewis' honor. His footprint is still there.

Oh, a large, thick slab of cement covers the well. They are the only two visible things that remain on the hill to prove a house was ever there.

The hill was neatly mowed. I could see scattered between the grass tiny moss roses growing. It was an impulse to dig one or two up, but there was no spade.

The cedar trees have grown to be giant trees—so tall and stately.

I used to think the sun was brighter there than anywhere else in the world. The same warm glow came over me a few weeks ago standing on that Hallowed land.

Virginia and I walked on the mowed grass until we came to weeds as tall as our waists. Both of us saw a thorny bush. We went right up to it and lo and behold, the bush had thorns all over it except the very tip of each branch. At the very tip of each thorny branch were the most vibrant dark purple blossoms. Hard to describe the color—wish I knew the name of that weed! The bees were all around the bush, busy drinking the nectar.

God's presence was with me while I stood in awe, examining this strange bush of beauty and evil (the thorns). God taught me a lesson right there: the bush represents the thorns we often have to endure in life but, oh, the beautiful purple blossoms more than make up for all of the thorns in life.

Mary Adelaide Webb Wray
On revisiting "The Hill" in Boydton, Virginia
Spring of 2000

MY TREASURES.

Ecclesiastes 3-19:21.

21- Who knowest the spirit of man that goeth upward, and the spirit of the beast that goeth downward to the earth?

"If only our hearts sing, the weight of the years is lifted."

_____Proverbs

St. Augustine wrote: "Thou hast made us for Thyself, and restless are our hearts, until they rest in Thee."

We can travel the world over in search for the beautiful, but unless we have it within our Souls, we find it not.

_____M.W.W.

Some scenery so beautiful, looking out over a scene so beautiful and serene is to be almost beyond belief.

_____M.W.W.

Uncle Robert once said. "Someone was as true as the needle is to a Pole."

"The Prince of peace." What a sweet name for our savior.

_____Isaiah 9-6

Hanging on the wall in my bedroom is a plaque. My sister Nell gave it to me. It describes love perfectly.......

Love is patient and kind;
Love is not jealous or boastful;
It is not arrogant or rude,
Love does not insist on its own way,
It is not irritable or resentful,
It does not rejoice at wrong,
but rejoices in the right,
Love bears all things
believes all things,
hopes ll things,
endures all things,
love never ends...

_____1-Corinthians 13:4-8

God gave the sea His decree.

_____Proverbs 8-29

When He gave to the sea His decree that the waters should not pass His commandments.
Psalm 33-7
Psalm 104-9

Jeremiah 5-22

Fear of death taken away:

Hebrews 2:15
And delivers them who through fear of death were all their lifetime subject to bondage.

The lost are separated from the saved by a great gulf fixed.

_____Luke 16-26

"Clouds of infinite color tones
A fore taste of the veiled glory to be,
revealed some day to startled eyes in
the land where we'll never grow old."

_____Auntie

Sometimes I know how Mary of Bethany must have felt when Jesus told those people to leave her alone, for she hath done what she could.

_____Mark 14-3:9

The precious blood of Christ runs like a red cord through the Bible (from Genesis through Revelation.)

_____M.W.W.

Psalm 116-15: Precious in the sight of the Lord is the death of His saints.

John 8-6:11 and read;
John 7:"He that is without sin among you, let him first cast a stone at her."

What a compassionate Savior! Brother Lewis and I always thought this is so sweet what Jesus said to this woman.
1 Timothy 6-7
God is not partial.

11 Timothy 3-16

All scripture is given by inspiration of God and is profitable for doctrine, for reproof, for correction, for instruction in righteousness.

Psalm 90-10
The days of our years are threescore years and ten; and if by reason of strength they be fourscore years, yet is their strength labour and sorrow; for it is soon cut off, and we fly away.

Happiness is when someone cares that really loves you. Oh! Happy Day!

___M.W.W.

NATIONS (ONLY MEN)

Psalms 9:20
Put them in fear, O LORD: that the nations may know themselves to be but men. Se Lah

Deep down in the very soul of lie there is an eternal law: the law of the cross.

Nothing we possess really belongs to us. Our time, talents, homes, money, personalities, even our very lives are given us as a trust. Now only does the God own the earth and all that is therein but, He owns mankind as well, since all things are His creation..

____M.W.W.

We must truly show our love for God whom we have not seen, when we love our brother whom we have seen.

____M.W.W.

Others are merely mirrors of you, You can not love or hate something about another person unless it reflects something you love or hate about yourself.

_____M.W.W.

1John 5:21. Little children, keep yourselves from idols.

The Bible is the Book of Books. The author is God. The theme is Christ.

_____M.W.W.

"The Master Builder is doing His best with the material that is being sent up."

_____M.W.W.

Dandelions: "Just a beautiful common weed that plagues every lawn or just about every lawn. Being so plentiful, they are a nuisance and not loved but let's suppose they were rare. Wouldn't they be nurtured in a flower garden?"

My dear sister, Virginia Webb Newman, wrote this several years ago.

Prayer is opening the door of your heart and letting God in.

_____Moody

No matter what suffering we endure, nothing compares to the suffering our Lord did for us He suffered everything.

_____M.W.W.

Read: Isaiah 52:14

In the Hand of the Lord, there is a cup and the wine is red.

_____M.W.W.

Lord, give me an understanding heart.

_____M.W.W.

We have to be Holy in order to go to Heaven, for Heaven is a Holy Place.

_____M.W.W.

Do you know the last thing that dies in a man? It is the love of self when it should be the love of God and Our Lord Savior, Jesus Christ.

_____M.W.W.

Angels: Physical safety and well-being of believers. Care of the heirs of salvation being in infancy and continues through life. Angels receive departing events.

_____M.W.W.

Everything that God's Finger's touch is beautiful.

_____M.W.W.

"Never try to love any more than you do. Just think of how much He loves you."

_____Anonymous

The more I serve Him, the sweeter He is.

_____M.W.W.

"We believe in Eternal life, we know his or her death is not the end but, knowing that does not ease the pain of a loss."

_____M.W.W.

MY Ole MY! So many so called Christians have said to me through the years, "Well Ms. Mary, I can hardly wait to go to Heaven but I do not want to go just yet." I guess they are afraid but I do not understand why.

_____M.W.W.

"God forbid that I should sin against the Lord in ceasing to pray for you."

____1: Samuel 12:23

"Root yourself deep in Him so that you may never forget that you are only the channel and He is the source."

_____M.W.W.

"And ever near us, though unseen
The dear immortal spirits tread;
for all the boundless universe is life,
There are no dead."

_____M.W.W.

Sunday morning, December 23, 1991
Reading my Bible this morning gives to me wings for my spirit. Yes, a divine help in necessary when I read my bible and the gates of light are opened.

Oh! How I would love for someone to take me to the seashore today and walk to a solitude place along the beach and meditate deeply to my dear Lord.

____M.W.W.

Ecclesiastes 3-19:21

POETRY

I am many things as I have much practice at this age in life. I do not claim to be a poet but there were thoughts on my mind and I wanted to put them in poetry form. I have two grandchildren who have served this country in another land several times now and I wanted to write this because of them and also for the others being in that desert sand and my heart goes out to all of the young men and women who defend our freedom.

Then I wanted to write one day a little something for my children so they can have something from my heart one day. I guess it is for all of God's little children.

O- STARS AND STRIPES

O-Stars and stripes o'er yonder,

Such glory amongst your boundary,

All around-battle after battle begins to occur,

A wounded soldier falls on one knee

While comforting his buddy on foreign desert sand

And clasping the flag of peace,

In a bloody crippled hand.

And as soldier's coat the white sand,

And stars and stripes wave silently,

Atop the dunes of foreign land,

Screams, confusion, pleas for mom,

Precious call to be free,

Then a distant cry, woman, men, men, woman

The U.S. Soldier, brave, courageous, proud,

Valiant soldiers dressed in armour,

guns, cannons, rockets, unbearable loud,

Piercing flashings of amber
Still, My God! Stars and stripes,

Wave peacefully, boldly, triumphantly,

Within the lonely desert sand.

To once again to let old life

become anew.

Be freed, succeed, believe, achieve,

O' stars and stripes; red, white and blue,

I remain; so proud of you.

_____M.W.W.

FOR MY CHILDREN

I'll be loving you always,
With a love that is true,
Yes, always, Yes, always;
When the things you plan,
Need a helping hand,
Your mom will understand,
Yes, always,
day's may not be fair to you but,
I will be close by, Yes, always,
Yes, that is when I will always
Not just for an hour,
Not just for a day,
No, not for just a year;
but always, I will love you.

_____M.W.W.

We come from good, strong, God-fearing stock and had many brilliant and eminent men and women in our long line. Never forget this, and be true to the religion of our forefathers. The greatest heritage that one can possess is a background of fine ancestors who have left a record of achievement, integrity, and uprightness.

So try to do your part in life and add luster to our honored name, trusting that you may always cherish this record of genealogy and all that our ancestors stood for.

Let us not forget what they stood for.

Mary Adelaide Webb Wray
1995

Try this:

When waking up in the morning, look up at the ceiling... the ceiling is so clean and is not cluttered...then look down at all of the clutter

Heaven and Earth

Isaiah 66:1

Thus saith the Lord, the Heaven is My Throne and the Earth is My footstool.

Matthew 6:19-20

19 – Lay not up for yourselves treasurer upon Earth, where moth and rust doth corrupt, and where thieves break through and steal.

20 – But lay up for yourselves treasures in Heaven.

"Love knows no season"
Mary Adelaide Webb Wray
December 2004

Yesterday, Today, and Tomorrow

There are two days in every week about which we should not worry, two days which should be kept free from fear and apprehension.

One of these days is **yesterday** with its mistakes and cares, its faults and blunders, its aches and pains. **Yesterday** has passed forever beyond our control.

Tomorrow's sun will rise, either in splendor or behind a mask of clouds, but it will rise. Until it does, we have no stake in **tomorrow**, for it is as yet unborn.

This leaves only one day—**today**. Any man can fight the battles of just one day. It is only when you and I add the burdens of those two awful eternities –**yesterday** and **tomorrow**—that we break down.

It is not the experience of today that drives men mad; it is remorse or bitterness for something which happened **yesterday** and the dread of what **tomorrow** may bring.

Let us, therefore, live but one day at a time.

Author Unknown

GOOD-BYE

My! I just hate good-byes. The same for so long. Why don't I just say; Until Another Day. This has been a fun adventure and hopefully someday my daughter will staple it together, run a few copies, and pass it out to a few family members. Then maybe I can say I have left something behind for others to enjoy. Then again they may throw it away in the trash. I only know I have done my very best at my age of 90 years to tell others something worthwhile about my family life as a child and as an adult. There are of course many things I did not say in these pages. I know them but at times I forget and so that venture will have to wait until another day.

How I am concerned about the young and also the elderly. The young are not sure what they want to do in life and I cannot blame them with these conditions in the world today. I honestly would not know how to counsel them today. But so many are good kids and all they need is a little coaching. The problem is many do not know how to coach! So we have a young person growing up in a world and for the most part many look the other way. Maybe if one reads just one little part of this book it may lead them to the right path in life. Maybe. A big word but it could happen at any hour.

Then we have the elderly or senior citizen, the one living in golden years, the one many people ignore. How unfair. Golden years. I wish I knew the person that started saying that sick statement. There is nothing golden about these years but one has to look for any bright spot to come their way and pray for another day. No, it makes no difference if it is cold or hot, or snowy or rainy. It is another day and all days are beautiful to me. Just like people, we have to look for the good in all human beings.

This final piece of this puzzle will complete this task for me. It has not been easy at all writing SWEET SOUTHERN DAYS but it has taught me so much about life.

Hey kids! Even at my age there is always something special I can learn about life. The important thing one wants to never forget, never give up or in to anything in life. Never let someone influence your precious mind as God has given you a special gift, the power of choice. You make that choice and live with it and at times it may be the wrong choice or it may be the right choice. Just stand behind your decision and if it proves to be the right choice then celebrate and if it proves to be the wrong choice then have broad enough shoulders to be the first to admit it. That is how one earns respect and how one is at peace.

I say to you one last quote; " Anything in life worthwhile is not easy." M.W.W. No, there has honestly been zilch that has been easy to come my way in life but it does not matter as my life has surely been worthwhile. I would never trade any of it. I have done my very best and most importantly my God knows it. But I do not like Good-Byes as I have mentioned so I will say ; Until Another Day. If God allows it. My love to all.

THE END

My mother, Mary Adelaide Webb Wray, took her last breath in the afternoon after a bout of illness on January 21, 2010 at her home she so dearly loved with her family by her side.

Frank Alexander Wray

Frank Alexander Wray and Mary Webb